CLEVER CATS!
Amazing Cat Adventures

Robyn P. Watts

KNOWLEDGE BOOKS

Teacher Notes:

Cats have been an important part of many peoples' lives around the world for thousands of years. However, as their numbers have increased, they have also started to threaten our wildlife. Learn more about the amazing characteristics of cats, how to look after them, and most importantly, how to protect our wildlife from these apex predators.

Discussion points for consideration:

1. Why has the wild cat population exploded in many country areas around the world?

2. Why is desexing and cat registration such a good idea in some places?

3. What is your favourite cat characteristic and why?

4. Do you think that there should be cat curfews? This means that cats are not allowed out at night or to leave a person's house.

Difficult words to be introduced and practiced before reading this book:

Antarctica, worldwide, America, mouser, comfort, popular, African, friendship, Ancient, Egyptians, special, protected, related, Leopard, ancestor, predator, distance, vision, pupil, apex, frequency, rotate, balance, canals, mammals, pierce, cushion, scent, medicine, regularly, environment, disappeared, wildlife, controlling, register.

Contents

1. About Cats

We all know cats. We see them at windows or out walking. Cats make good pets. Do you have a cat as a pet? Do you want a cat? This book will help with your questions.

Cats have been with people for a long time. The only place where there are no cats is Antarctica. Worldwide, there are about one billion cats. Some of these are wild cats and the rest are pets.

The top cat lovers are North America, Japan, China, and Russia. All sorts of people own cats, from leaders of countries, to the young and old, and the rich and poor. Cats are cute, cuddly, and easy to look after.

In America, cats have been kept at the White House. President Clinton kept a cat called Socks. It was a black and white cat and lived at the White House.

In the United Kingdom, a cat is kept at the house of the Prime Minister as a mouser. The cats have become very famous. Many stories have been told about them. Larry was a tabby cat kept by the Prime Minister of the UK. Larry even showed up for a meeting with the President of the United States of America.

5

Cats go to many workplaces. They help to get rid of pests like rats, mice, and birds. Some schools have cats in classrooms to stop rats and mice.

People love to see their cats at work. Cats make friends with people and bring them happiness. They give comfort to people who are worried or sad. This makes it a happier place for everyone.

Cats love to play. They do funny things that make people laugh. They sit on desks and chairs. They even climb on screens and on to people.

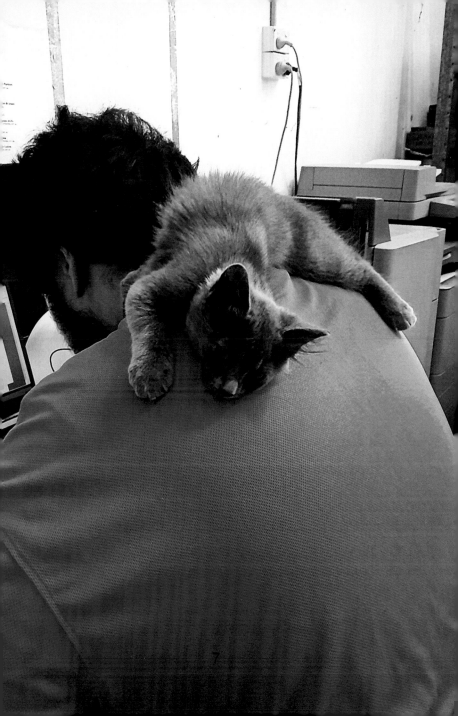

Today, cats are found in every country. Cats were taken to these countries. They did not always live there. People brought the cats as pets to stop rats and mice. Today, they are the second most popular pet after dogs.

Some of these cats went wild and lived in the cities and forests. Today, these wild cats live off small animals and food scraps from people. The number of wild cats across the whole world would be huge.

2. Cats Are Everywhere

Many years ago, cats did not live all over the world. They came from the dry deserts and mountains of North Africa. They climbed trees easily and were expert hunters.

The wild African cat looks like our cats today. There has been little change in their head shape. They still have strong, fast legs to help them hunt.

Cats started living near people when rats turned up to eat the grain. The rats ate the grain and people began starving. Cats were happy to eat the rats which left the grain for the people. This is how a long friendship started.

Ancient Egyptians thought that the cat was special. The rulers of Egypt had cats in their palaces. The cats were very important animals. They protected people by killing rats and snakes.

You can see paintings of cats on the walls of temples and tombs in Egypt. The Egyptians thought cats had special powers and looked after the people.

What are cats related to? Most of the big cats and other cats are related to the cats of today. The wild Leopard Cat of China is a close relative to today's cats.

Cats are also related to lions, leopards, and other big cats. There was a common ancestor millions of years ago. Some of these cats grew large, and others grew into smaller animals. They are all predators and only eat meat.

panthera

bay cat

caracal

ocelot

lynx

puma

Asian leopard cat

domestic cat

3. Looking at Cats

Cats have big eyes which makes them look very cute. Wild cats also have the same big eyes. They help the cat to hunt at night in very low light.

The eyes of the cat are very special. Look at the skull of the cat's head. The eye socket is very big. The eyes can see small things from a great distance.

Cats hunt at night when it's dark. People need to wear night vision goggles to see things at night. Cats can see without these googles. A cat can open and close its pupil to help it see better in the dark. It can see 10 times better than people in the dark.

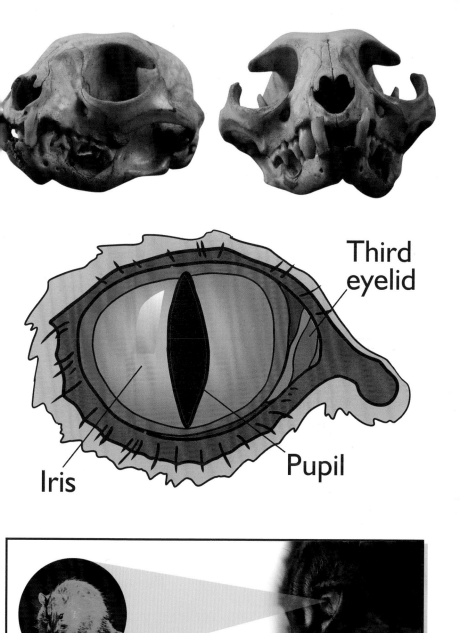

Third eyelid

Iris

Pupil

Night Vision

Cats are called 'apex' killers. 'Apex' means the very top. Cats are so good at hunting that they can spend most of the day sleeping and cleaning their fur. They don't need much time for hunting because they find and kill their prey easily.

Hearing is important for a cat. They listen for squeaks from mice and rats. Cats hear sounds at a higher frequency that humans can't hear. They also have ears that move around to follow sounds. This helps them to find their prey.

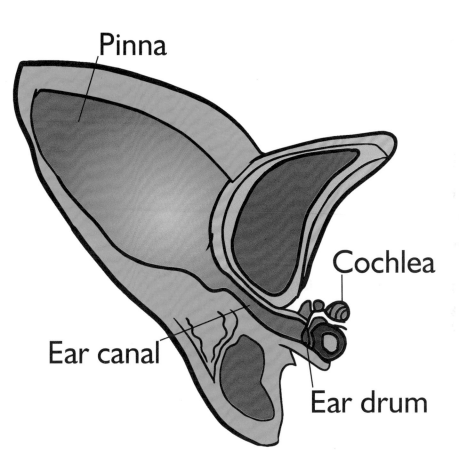

Pinna

Cochlea

Ear canal

Ear drum

Cats have amazing balance. They can climb trees easily. They can leap up to nine times their length into the air. They can leap across rocks and trees.

Cats always seem to land on all four paws. This great balance comes from inside a cat's ears. A cat has four canals inside its ears. Sometimes cats get stuff in their ears. If this is not cleaned out by a vet, it can affect their balance.

Cats are mammals. This means that cats give birth to live babies. They do not lay an egg like a bird. Cats give milk to their young.

All mammals like cats have fur. Fur is important as cats are warm-blooded. The fur helps to keep their body warm.

Cats have kittens. Each litter can be up to 7 kittens. Cats breed very quickly and can have three litters in a year. This means wild cats can grow in number very fast.

Cats in the wild can kill many birds and other small animals like lizards. Look at the cat skull and its large fangs. All cats have these big fangs. They help to cut, pierce, and tear muscle and skin. Cats use these fangs to cut off the neck bones in rats and mice.

The bones of a cat are special too! The bones have a soft cushion at the joints. This helps the cat when jumping. It can land easily on its pads without being hurt.

The backbone of the cat is curved. It can be rolled up like a rope. A cat can sleep curled up in a tiny space.

25

Cats can smell 40 times better than people. They mark their area by rubbing their scent against people, trees, and other things. They know if another cat has marked those areas. This can sometimes cause fights.

A cat's nose is full of nerve cells that help it to smell even tiny things. Inside the roof of their mouth there are more smell senses. These pick up special scent smells from other cats. Cats can also tell if their food is not fresh – they are not just being fussy!

In the wild, cats can smell other animals over 3 miles away. It can track an animal to where it is hiding. It waits quietly for the animal to come out before it attacks. Cats would make great tracking animals if they would only do what they were told!

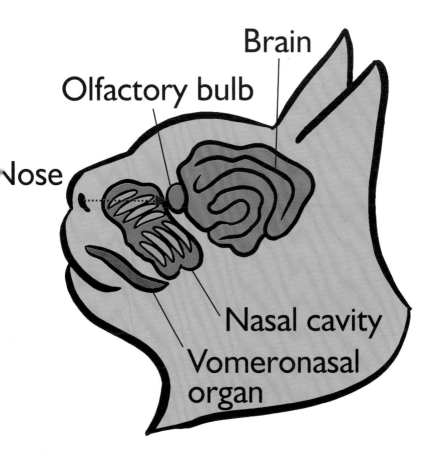

Brain

Olfactory bulb

Nose

Nasal cavity

Vomeronasal
organ

4. Looking After Cats

Cats can be great pets, but they need care. They need to have fresh, clean water every day. They need to be treated for fleas and ticks. You need to brush their fur to remove burrs and tangles.

You should not feed cats bread, cookies, or milk. They can't break down these foods. The only good food for a cat is fresh meat like fish or chicken.

Cats can get worms which live in their stomach. They need regular worm medicine. Cats also need a fresh box of clean litter for their toilet. All these things help keep them healthy.

Cats have special claws. You can't always see these claws. They only come out when a cat jumps to grab onto something. The claws are very sharp, like fishhooks.

When cats play, they usually don't have their claws out. If they did, they would scratch your skin. Some people worry about a cat's claws and will ask a vet to remove them. This is cruel and stops the cat from climbing and jumping safely. Declawing is banned in many countries. Never let anyone do this to your cat!

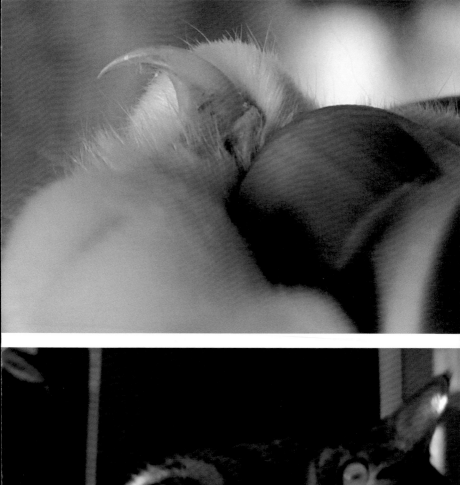

5. Cats as Pets

Can cats and dogs be friends? Yes, but you must be careful! Dogs and cats fear each other at first. It may take time for them to get to know each other and build trust.

Dogs like to chase cats and cats like to scratch dogs. You need to stop this from happening. Let the dog and cat meet slowly. Let them see each other through a glass window. After a while let them be in the same area. After a few days the cat will get closer to the dog.

Dogs and cats will play together and have fun. It is very funny to watch a cat and dog chasing a ball together. After they become friends, the cat and dog will even sleep together to stay warm.

Are cats bad for the environment? Pet cats and wild cats are apex predators and kill other animals. Lizards and birds are very easy for a cat to kill. Cats will kill all sorts of beautiful birds.

Wild cats kill billions of small animals across the world. Many animals have disappeared forever due to cats. Birds, lizards, bats, small moles, and other animals – all gone! The cat is the number one killer of wildlife. If you live in a beautiful nature area, do not get a cat!

If you want a cat, make sure it is kept in the house. Do not let it out to hunt at night or early in the morning. If you have a small yard, try to get a cat run so it can be outside without killing birds.

Some places have rules about controlling cats, like:

- Do not let your cat off your property.

- Do not let your cat outside at night.

- Tag and register your cat.

- Do not let your cat kill wildlife.

These rules are important for your cat and for the wildlife!

37

6. Training Cats

Can you train a cat? Yes, cats can be trained. A cat is a smart animal. They may not seem interested like a dog. Cats need to know there is a food reward.

The first one is easy. When the cat is being fed, ask the cat to 'sit!' When the cat sits, you can then feed the cat. The cat will quickly learn that food and 'sit' go together.

The next one is to chase a ball or rolled up piece of paper. The cat will 'fetch' but will need to be trained to bring the ball back. When the cat drops the ball in your hand, reward it with some food.

Cats are a lot of fun for so many people. They are fun to watch and make many people happy. Cats also do good by keeping rats and mice away.

There are lots of different cat colors, sizes, and breeds. Before getting a cat, you need to think about these things:

- Can I feed it three times a day?

- Can I get fresh food for the cat?

- Can I stop it from getting outside to kill animals?

- Can I keep my cat healthy, busy, happy, and safe?

If you can do all these things, then it may be time to have your very own cat!